Frederick Banting

Discoverer of Insulin

EDITORIAL DEVELOPMENT BY MICHAEL WEBB

ACCESS NO: 9126657

Copp Clark Pitman Ltd.
A Longman Company

C0-BWZ-871

©Copp Clark Pitman Ltd. 1991

All rights reserved. No part of this work covered by the copyrights hereon may be reproduced or used in any form or by any means — graphic, electronic, or mechanical — without the prior written permission of the publisher.

Any request for photocopying, recording, taping, or for storing on information storage and retrieval systems of any part of this book shall be directed in writing to the Canadian Reprography Collective, 379 Adelaide Street West, Suite M1, Toronto, Ontario M5V 1S5.

ISBN 0-7730-5053-1 (Casebound) ISBN 0-7730-5054-X (Paperback)

Canadian Cataloguing in Publication Data
Main entry under title:
Frederick Banting, discoverer of insulin

(Scientists & inventors series)
ISBN 0-7730-5053-1 (bound) ISBN 0-7730-5054-X (pbk.)

1. Banting, F.G. (Frederick Grant), Sir, 1891–1941 — Juvenile literature. 2. Diabetes — Research — Canada — Juvenile literature. 3. Medical scientists — Canada — Biography — Juvenile literature. 4. Physicians — Canada — Biography — Juvenile literature. I. Webb, Michael, 1949–   . II. Series.

R464.B3F7 1991   j616.4'62027'092   C90-095373-X

MICHAEL WEBB, a former school teacher and chemistry professor, now works as an editor and writer in Toronto. He has a doctorate in chemistry from the University of Alberta.

RESEARCH: *Jo Mrozewski*
EDITING AND PHOTO RESEARCH: *Grace D'Alfonso*
DESIGN AND ART DIRECTION: *Susan Hedley*
TYPESETTING: *Sonja Mills Graphic Arts Inc.*
PRINTING AND BINDING: *Friesen Printers Ltd.*

ACKNOWLEDGEMENTS
Many thanks to Francesca Verre, aged 11, for reading the manuscript.

PHOTO AND ILLUSTRATION CREDITS
F.G. Banting Papers, Thomas Fisher Rare Book Library, University of Toronto: cover, iv, 2, 3, 5, 6, 7, 13, 14, 16, 17, 20, 25; *Connaught Laboratories Limited:* 10, 21; *Malcolm Cullen:* 8, 11, 23; *IMS Creative Communications:* 4, 15, 19, 22; *Jeremy Jones:* 9; *MediSense, Inc.:* 24; *Medi-Serv:* 18; *Ontario Science Centre:* 12; *J. Wood/Miller Comstock:* 1.

Copp Clark Pitman Ltd., 2775 Matheson Blvd. East,
Mississauga, Ontario L4W 4P7

Printed and bound in Canada.

CONTENTS

Dr. Frederick Banting.

ɪNTRODUCTION

Are you a **diabetic**? If you are, you may owe your life to a Canadian scientist, Dr. Frederick Grant Banting. If you are not a diabetic, perhaps you have a friend or relative who is.

Diabetes is a very serious disease. But, because of Banting's work, millions of lives have been saved. With the proper treatment, diabetics can now lead fairly normal, active lives.

But what was Banting's great discovery? It was a drug called **insulin**.

Banting's work has saved millions of lives.

Who Was Frederick Banting?

People in Fred's home town, Alliston, Ontario, never thought that he would be famous. He wasn't very different from other people.

Fred was born on November 14, 1891. His parents were successful farmers, and Fred grew up on the farm. Though he was the youngest of six children, Fred had to do his share of the work. He often did the unpleasant job of cleaning the hen houses.

The Banting farmhouse.

Fred's parents made sure that he learned to value hard work and education. But Fred started out hating school. Because he was a farm boy, he felt miserable and out of place in a town school.

Even with lots of study, Fred did not get very good marks. He even had to repeat some exams to graduate from high school!

Young Fred and his older brother.

UNIVERSITY DAYS

Fred's brothers bought a farm with money left by their grandfather. But Fred decided to go to the University of Toronto. He was thinking of becoming a teacher, but his parents wanted him to be a **minister**.

Though he tried hard in his first year, Fred did not do well. He was unsure of what he should study. After a lot of thought, he decided to be a doctor. So, in his second year at the University, he began to study medicine. Fred worked very hard to become a **surgeon**, but he was still not a very good student.

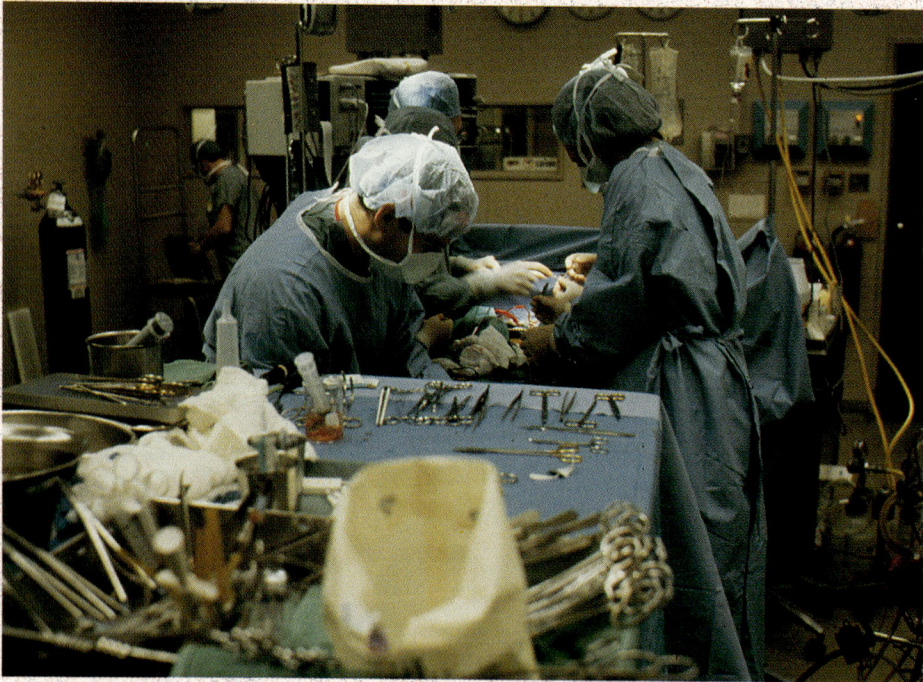

A surgeon at work today.

HOSP. TRAIN
MY DEAREST MOTHER 29/9/18
THIS LETTER WILL B SHORT
LEFT HAND. I WAS SLIGHTLY
WOUNDED YESTERDAY IN THE
RIGHT FOREARM. HAD
OPERATION LAST NIGHT
AND SHRAPNEL
SIZE REMOVED
FROM BETWEEN BONES.
NO FRACTURE BUT KIN A
BONE DAMAGED. I FEEL
PETTY GOOD.

ONLY TIRED.
I HAVE JUST HAD A BIG
HOT LOVELY DINNER
EVERY ONE IS AS KIND AS
CAN BE NOW PLEASE
DONT WORRY, I AM THE
LUCKIST BOY IN FRANCE.
I DONT KNOW WHERE
I AM GOING. ADDRESS
AS USUAL.
WITH LOVE
FROM
FRED

Fred was tall, strong, and good at sports. He really liked baseball. Though he was shy, he had a girlfriend, Edith Roach. She had grown up with Fred in Alliston and was also at the University.

Fred planned to graduate in 1917, but **World War I** ended his studies. The army needed doctors, so Fred's class worked through the summer of 1916 to finish the course quickly.

Captain Fred Banting was a doctor in the **front lines** in France. One day, he was wounded in the arm, but he carried on working. He got a medal for being so brave.

After he was wounded, Fred wrote home with his "wrong" hand. (Can you write with your "wrong" hand?)

5

YOUNG DOCTOR BANTING

Dr. Banting's return to Canada was not easy. He worked briefly at the Hospital for Sick Children in Toronto to finish his medical training. He was unsure of what to do next.

Banting set up his medical practice in London, Ontario. It was a growing city with a medical school. At first, the new doctor had very few patients. In fact, in his first month, he made only four dollars. He had to sell his car.

Edith, by now his fiancée, was teaching nearby in Ingersoll. But Dr. Banting felt lonely in London and was worried about his work. To ease his **depression**, he took up painting. For the rest of his life, it was his favourite hobby.

Banting's painting called "Medicine Lake."

To fill his time and earn extra money, Banting began to teach medicine and do **research** at the University of Western Ontario. One of the talks he gave changed his life. It was a talk on diabetes.

Banting's painting called "Miners' Houses."

WHAT IS DIABETES?

You probably hear a lot about sugar. First you're told that your body needs it to move, grow, and live. Then you're told not to eat so many candy bars because sugar is bad for you. How can sugar be both good and bad for you?

Your body uses sugar as **fuel**. You get sugar by eating foods that contain it, such as fruits and candy bars. Or you can eat foods that contain **starch**. Examples are bread and potatoes. Your body changes starch into sugar. You must be careful to give your body the right amounts of sugar and starch.

Foods such as bread and fruit give your body the fuel it needs.

A sign of diabetes is a great thirst.
Of course, everyone gets thirsty sometimes.

If your body has too much or too little sugar and starch in a day, you may feel anxious or depressed and restless or sleepy. But some people have a much more serious problem. It is a disease called **diabetes mellitus**, often just called diabetes. Some people are born with it, but it can develop at any age.

People with serious cases of diabetes cannot use the sugar in their blood. Two signs of diabetes are a great thirst and a large amount of urine. The blood and urine of untreated diabetics are full of unused sugar.

THE SEARCH FOR A CURE

When Fred Banting became a doctor, diabetes had been known for hundreds of years. There was no cure. Children with the disease usually died within a few years. Some adults with mild cases could survive by eating very little sugar and starch.

A special diet, called the Allen diet, helped many diabetics live longer. Patients ate as little as they possibly could to stay alive. They faced the horrible choice of quickly dying of diabetes or slowly starving to death.

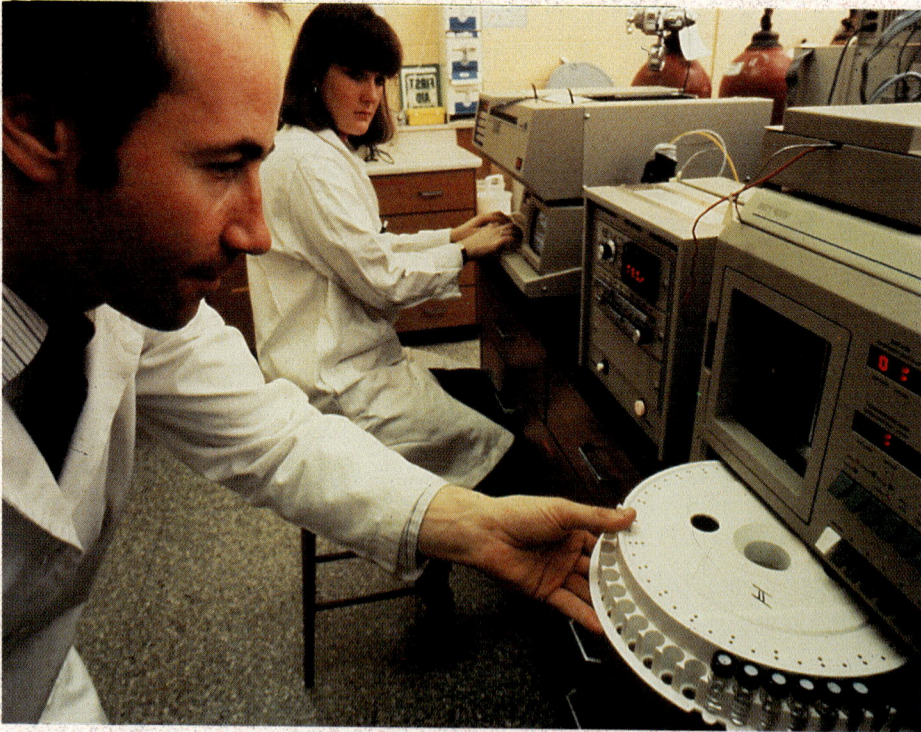

Many workers are trying to learn more about diabetes.

This picture shows where your pancreas is.

Many workers tried to understand and cure the disease. As usual in science, each worker added a little more knowledge. Before Banting began his own work, researchers knew that damaging or removing the **pancreas** caused diabetes. But they did not know why.

One of the top scientists working on diabetes at that time was Dr. J.J.R. Macleod at the University of Toronto. Fred Banting was soon to meet him.

BANTING'S RESEARCH

The room that Banting and Best worked in looked like this.

On October 31, 1920, Dr. Banting prepared his talk on the pancreas and diabetes. That night, he read an article that gave him an idea. So he visited Dr. Macleod in Toronto. The first meeting did not go well. In fact, Dr. Macleod thought that Fred Banting knew little about research.

But the young doctor was stubborn. He eventually convinced Dr. Macleod to support the research. Banting started his experiments at the University of Toronto on May 17, 1921. He was given a very poorly equipped room, some dogs, and an assistant named Charles Best. The dogs were to be used for research. A month after the work began, Dr. Macleod left to spend the summer in Scotland.

Banting, the surgeon, operated on the dogs. In some cases, he removed the pancreas to cause diabetes. In other cases, he left the pancreas in place but performed an operation that made it **wither**. Best tested the blood and urine of all the dogs for sugar.

Most of the early operations failed. Many dogs died of infections. But, after a few weeks, Banting and Best removed the withered pancreases from two dogs. They made an **extract** of withered pancreas. Then, with a needle, they injected the extract into dogs whose pancreases had been removed. Some dogs improved for a short time but then died. Finally, Banting and Best managed to keep a dog alive for three weeks.

Banting and Best with one of their dogs.

13

SUCCESS!

Banting checking one of the dogs.

Dr. Macleod returned and made many valuable suggestions. He knew that the work would have to be good enough to convince any scientist in the world.

After months of work, Banting and Best found that they could keep dogs alive with an extract of beef pancreas. So, the pancreas extract did not need to come from other dogs. Also, the pancreas did not have to be withered for its extract to work. Banting's original idea had been wrong.

Dr. James Collip, an experienced **biochemist**, joined the team. He found ways to improve the extract and test how strong it was. But the members of the team were not always friendly with each other. Banting felt that Collip was competing with him and that Macleod was taking too much credit for the work. Though they did not always get along well, they all carried on working together.

After more setbacks, tests of the beef pancreas extract began on human diabetics. The extract worked! Macleod named this new drug "insulin."

It had taken nine months from Banting's first experiment to the reliable production of insulin. A year later, it was being used to treat humans. This major research project had taken an amazingly short period of time.

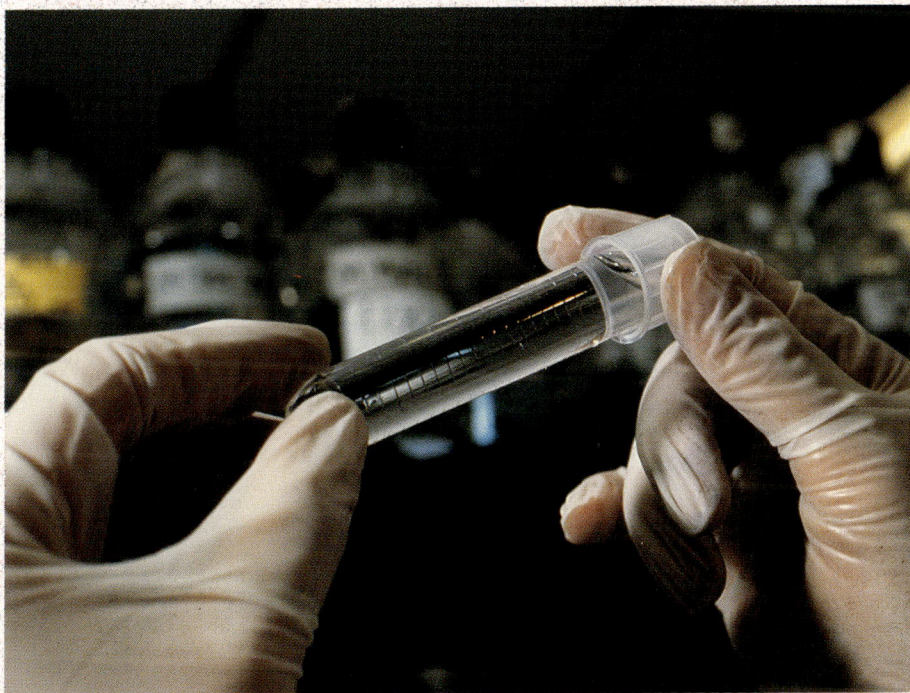

A container of insulin.

BANTING BECOMES FAMOUS

Many doctors, including Banting himself, spent several years finding out how best to treat patients with insulin. But, almost from the start, it saved lives and restored health.

Reports of success created worldwide interest almost overnight. By the end of 1922, diabetics were flocking to Toronto for treatment. Doctors were waiting for insulin supplies. By early 1923, insulin was being used in many cities across Canada and the United States.

Banting gave many newspaper interviews, though he did not like reporters. During the rest of his life, he made many speeches and special appearances. He also received many letters of thanks from grateful patients whose lives had been saved.

Countless awards followed. The most important was the **Nobel Prize** in Medicine. In 1923, this was awarded to Banting and Macleod for the discovery of insulin. Banting was furious that Macleod, and not Charles Best, shared the award with him.

Banting's share of the Nobel Prize was $20 000, a large sum of money at the time. He gave half to Charles Best. Macleod split his own share with James Collip.

Dr. J.J.R. Macleod.

Dr. James Collip.

The Nobel Prize won by Banting and Macleod in 1923.

THE MIRACLE DRUG

It is hard to imagine the impact of the discovery of insulin. The drug's effects on severe diabetics seemed like a miracle. Some looked like living skeletons and could hardly move. Within weeks of treatment with insulin, they began to put on weight and look much healthier.

Injecting insulin.

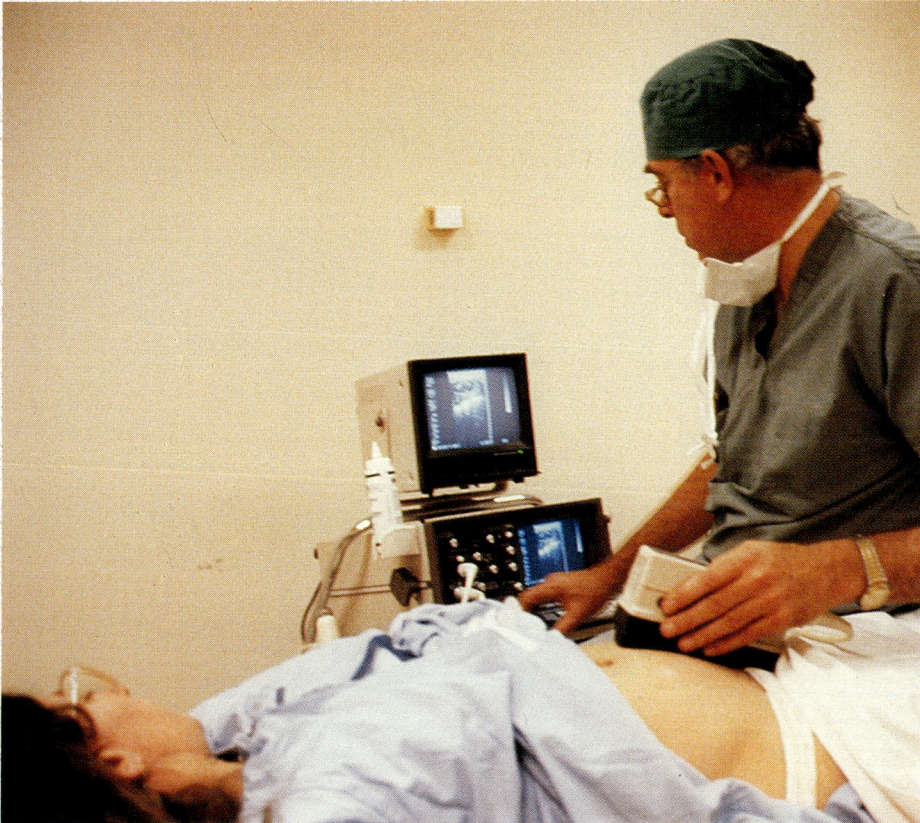

Diabetic women can have healthy children.

Since 1922, millions of lives have been saved by insulin. Before insulin treatment, severe diabetics could not be operated on. Their bodies were too fragile to cope with the shock of surgery. Today, diabetics are operated on with few problems.

Without insulin treatment, severely diabetic women could not have children. Diabetes would harm, or even kill, the mother or baby. Some diabetic women still have problems today, but most can be treated successfully. Many diabetic women have healthy children.

Banting's
Other Achievements

The Banting Institute.

Banting's achievements were not all in the **laboratory**. He had an important effect on science in Canada. His work made people realize that scientific research was important. Suddenly, there was more money and support for young scientists than ever before.

The University of Toronto set up the Banting Research Foundation and the Banting Institute. So money became available for Banting and other scientists to do medical research.

Banting himself donated money to research, including the part of the Nobel Prize he had not given to Charles Best. The **patent** for the production of insulin could have made Banting very wealthy. But he sold the patent to the University of Toronto for one dollar, so that the drug could be made as cheaply as possible.

In 1914, the University had started a company, Connaught Laboratories. It made **vaccines** as well as treatments for poisoning. However, Connaught became important when it started to make insulin. So the insulin story is a good example of how science and business can work together for everyone's good.

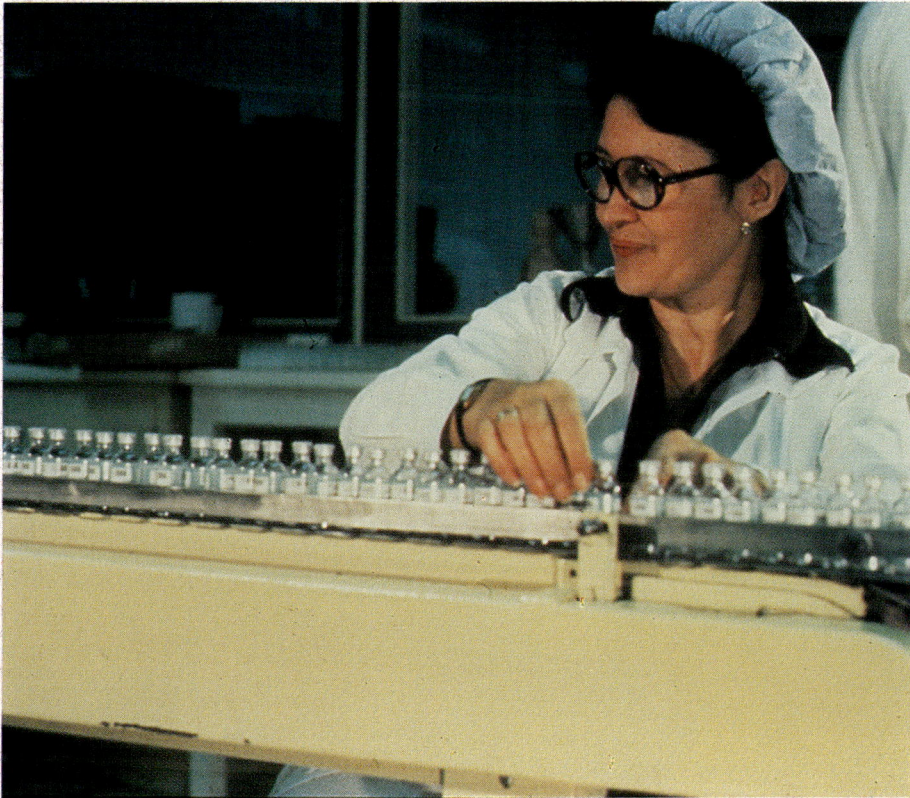

Making insulin at Connaught Laboratories.

Banting's Later Years

After getting the Nobel Prize, Banting worked as hard as ever. He spent much of his time supervising other people's research, and helping governments and medical groups. He was so busy that he could not spend as much time on his own research, which he thought of as his real work.

Banting never did repeat the success he had with insulin. He was always fascinated by the idea of other **secretions** that might cure diseases. Yet his training and skill were in surgery, not in biochemistry.

In his personal life, Banting's engagement to Edith Roach had ended in May, 1924. He soon married Marion Robertson, an **X-ray technician** at Toronto General Hospital. They had a son in 1929, but the marriage was not a success.

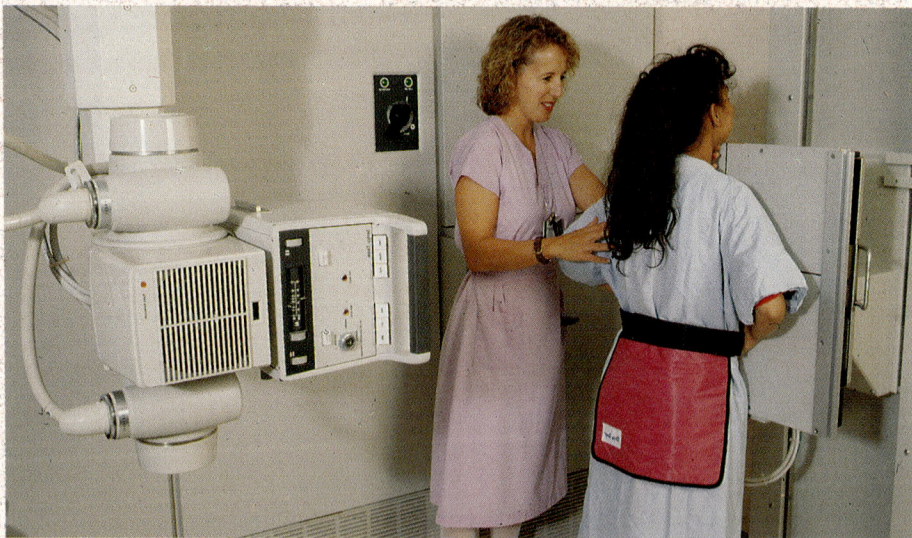

An X-ray technician at work.

The Bantings divorced in 1932. In those days, divorce was quite shocking, so there was a great deal of bad publicity. Though Dr. Banting wanted a happy family life, he did not marry again until 1939. His second wife was Henrietta Ball, who did medical research herself.

When **World War II** started in 1939, Banting volunteered for wartime research. Toward the end of 1940, he arranged a trip to England to exchange information. On February 21, 1941, his plane took off from Gander airport in Newfoundland. A few minutes later, the plane crashed in the bush northeast of Gander. Dr. Frederick Grant Banting, Canada's most famous medical researcher, died of his injuries the following day.

Banting's plane crashed in Newfoundland.

Diabetes Today

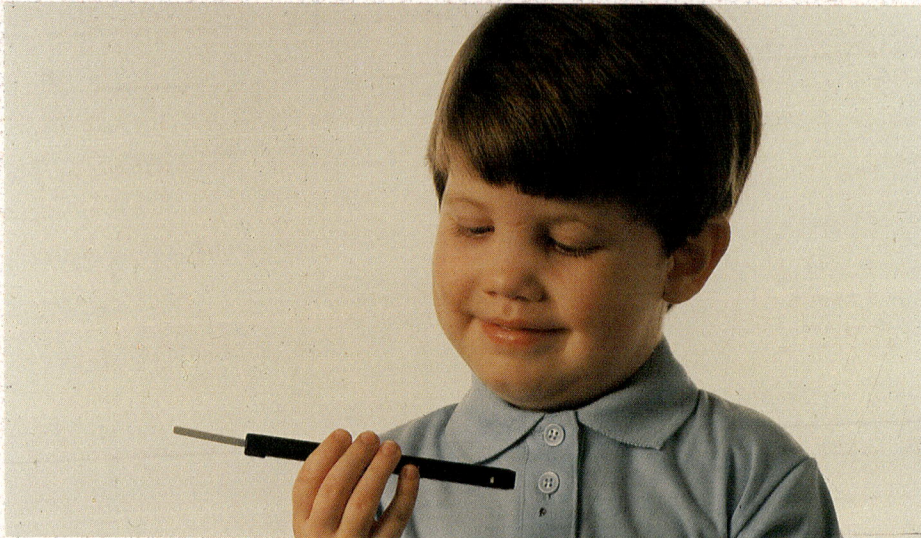

A diabetic child testing his blood.

The number of cases of diabetes continues to increase. About one person in 20 in North America is diabetic. Most diabetics can control the disease by eating and exercising sensibly. But about one in 200 North Americans has the severe form that requires daily injections of insulin.

People with severe cases of the disease must also be careful about what they eat. They need a well-balanced diet, with the right amount of sugar. They must be aware of the amount of food they need and when they should eat it. For example, they may need an extra snack before they exercise. Sensible eating habits and exercise help control the amount of sugar in the blood. Thanks to modern medicine, diabetics can now test the sugar in their blood every day to make sure that it is at a safe level.

Much of the insulin used in medicine still comes from the pancreases of animals. Pork pancreas is now used, as well as the beef pancreas used by Banting. However, some diabetics now inject **synthetic insulin**.

It may surprise you to learn that, despite all the research on diabetes, there is still no cure. Scientists do not yet understand the exact causes of the disease. However, there is hope that more research may soon tell us how to prevent or cure it. In the meantime, Banting's drug, insulin, keeps many diabetics alive.

Many people owe their lives to Dr. Frederick Banting.

GLOSSARY

biochemist — A scientist who studies certain kinds of changes that go on inside living things. *(p. 15)*

depression — A feeling of sadness that can make you feel tired and lazy. *(p. 6)*

diabetic — A person who suffers from **diabetes**. *(p. 1)*

diabetes — The common name for **diabetes mellitus**. *(p. 1)*

diabetes mellitus — A serious disease with no cure. Severe cases can kill if left untreated. Some people who have the disease for a long time get other problems, such as heart disease. *(p. 9)*

extract — A liquid that holds part of something. (Hot tea holds part of the tea leaves it was made from. So hot tea is an extract of tea leaves.) *(p. 13)*

front lines — The region in which enemy armies are closest together and the worst fighting takes place. *(p. 5)*

fuel — A material that lets something grow or move. (Gasoline is fuel for a car. Food is fuel for your body.) *(p. 8)*

insulin — A material that lets the body use sugar. Most people use their own insulin from the **pancreas**. People with severe **diabetes mellitus** must take insulin every day. *(p. 1)*

laboratory — A room where scientists do experiments. *(p. 20)*

minister — A person who runs a religious service in a church. *(p. 4)*

Nobel Prize — One of the world's top awards. There are Nobel Prizes for medicine, sciences, helping world peace, and other types of work. *(p. 16)*

pancreas — The part of the body that makes **insulin**. *(p. 11)*

patent — A way you can register an invention or discovery, so that you are the only person with the right to make or sell it for a certain number of years. *(p. 21)*

research — Work done to find out and explain new facts. *(p. 7)*

secretions — Materials made by parts of animals and plants. (When a baby dribbles, the liquid from its mouth is a secretion.) *(p. 22)*

starch — The form in which plants store sugar. When we eat plants, our bodies change the starch into sugar. *(p. 8)*

surgeon — A doctor who treats diseases and injuries by operating on people. (If you have had your appendix or tonsils removed, the work was done by a surgeon.) *(p. 4)*

synthetic insulin — Like the insulin that comes from animals, but made by companies from chemicals instead. *(p. 25)*

vaccines — Treatments given to people and animals to stop them from getting certain diseases. *(p. 21)*

wither — Shrink and dry up. (Cut flowers wither after a few days.) *(p. 13)*

World War I — The war from 1914 to 1918. Germany and other countries were on one side. The United Kingdom and other countries, including Canada, were on the other side. *(p. 5)*

World War II — The war from 1939 to 1945. It started with Germany and Italy against the United Kingdom and other countries, including Canada. Many other countries joined the War later. *(p. 23)*

X-ray technician — An operator of a machine that shows the bones inside the human body. *(p. 22)*

INDEX

1 2 3 4 5   5053-1   95 94 93 92 91
1 2 3 4 5   5054-X   95 94 93 92 91